SIGNS AND WONDERS
The True Miracles of Jesus

Renewing of my Mind
Repenting with my Words
Believing in my Heart

Alicia Buxton

First published by Ultimate World Publishing 2025
Copyright © 2025 Alicia Buxton

ISBN

Paperback: 978-1-923425-17-0
Ebook: 978-1-923425-18-7

Alicia Buxton has asserted her rights under the Copyright, Designs and Patents Act 1988 to be identified as the author of this work. The information in this book is based on the author's experiences and opinions. The publisher specifically disclaims responsibility for any adverse consequences which may result from use of the information contained herein. Permission to use information has been sought by the author. Any breaches will be rectified in further editions of the book.

All rights reserved. No part of this publication may be reproduced, stored in or introduced into a retrieval system, or transmitted in any form, or by any means (electronic, mechanical, photocopying, recording or otherwise) without the prior written permission of the author. Any person who does any unauthorised act in relation to this publication may be liable to criminal prosecution and civil claims for damages. Enquiries should be made through the publisher.

Cover design: Ultimate World Publishing
Layout and typesetting: Ultimate World Publishing
Editor: Victoria Pickens

Ultimate World Publishing
Diamond Creek,
Victoria Australia 3089
www.writeabook.com.au

Testimonial

An easy to read, interesting, honestly written story about Alicia's life, and the miracles that she received. She is courageous to admit to what has been some unacceptable aspects of her life, and shows how she achieved spiritual growth, which transformed her life.

Her warmth, kindness and dedication towards assisting others shines throughout this book.

Lorraine Freeman

Dedication

I wholeheartedly dedicate this book to my children, Victoria and Charles, and my granddaughters, Eden and Liv.

I also dedicated this book to the lukewarm believers, non-believer, Atheists and Agnostics, and those people who don't believe that Jesus Christ and the Blessed Virgin Mary exist.

I hope and pray that, after reading my book, they believe and repent in a way, and that they be the light of God to others.

Contents

Testimonial	iii
Dedication	v
Introduction	1
Chapter 1: What is the Name?	7
Chapter 2: What is Penance?	15
Chapter 3: Miracle of Obedience	21
Chapter 4: The Miracle of Courage	27
Chapter 5: Miracle of Blessing	33
Chapter 6: Miracle of Wonder	37
Chapter 7: Alicia's Revelation	43
Chapter 8: Miracle of Heaven and Hell	51
Chapter 9: Miracle of Devotion	57
Chapter 10: Miracle of Giving	63
Chapter 11: Miracle Signs	67
Chapter 12: Miracle of Love and Sufferance	73
Final Chapter: What is Next?	81
About the Author	89
Acknowledgement	93
Testimonials	95
Offers	97
Speaker Bio	99

Introduction

HOW IT ALL STARTED
MY REBIRTH

INTRODUCTION

This book is about the miracles that happened in my life, and I would like to share them with others.

Nothing is definite. I was happily married for twenty-four years, complacently doing my role as a dedicated mother and wife, until temptation came my way and changes came into being. I decided to divorce my loving, hardworking and devoted husband, and father of my two beautiful children.

I thought there was more to life than work and being a good housewife, which I then considered to be monotonous and boring. Since my children were starting their own lives, I thought I also wanted a bigger, better, and fun-filled life of my own. I wanted time to enjoy and discover the world. I wanted time for a change, so I decided to amicably leave everything and start what I thought would be a life that I did not have before.

Having attained my earlier dreams and goals of having my own businesses and being capable of living independently, I thought that this was the time to start a new beginning. But I was so, so wrong.

I was divorced in 2000, and I succumbed to living six years of "bliss" and sinfulness as I can describe it now.

I had never before had so much partying, late nights, and socialising in my life. I danced my life away. I thought, *this is living*! I was being sucked into all the 'bad things' – like alcohol, drugs, gambling, sex and bad company.

But thank God I wasn't fully deluded, and Mother Mary rescued me in 2006. Something in me—I suppose it was my culture or my upbringing—told me I did not really like these things.

My eyes were opened, I didn't and still don't like the taste of alcohol. I never had drugs before, as Mum told us when we were young that if we touched any marijuana (which was readily available then) or any kind of illegal drugs during my time at home, she would disown us. This was imprinted in my young brain as I was growing up. The only gambling machine I knew was the poker machine, and it was not my forte as I found it boring. I would rather play Scrabble for a challenge.

I tried having boyfriends, just like a blooming rose. I tried almost all the dating sites and began wasting my time and effort trying to find a decent date, but it was becoming hopeless. At one point, I thought it was pouring men. *Alleluia*, I thought, but I was wrong.

Looking back on my six years of sinful experience, I felt wasted and disgusted. "Been there, done that," I said to myself. Luckily, I am out. I feel sorry for and pray intently for those people who were sucked in and addicted and especially for those who are still there. I learnt my lessons;

INTRODUCTION

something I know to be true. I repented and promised God never to do it again. I am so grateful to Mama Mary for her intercession and for my rebirth and transformation. Without the miracle of me seeing Her with my own two eyes, I would not be a believer in action.

Looking back at my pampered life, which included business successes, financial stability, and the power to have everything I always wanted at my fingertips, I felt like I was on top of the world. I had everything I wanted and dreamed of, so I asked myself, "What is next?"

I thought to myself: *What other things do I need?* I examined my thoughts and asked myself, "What is the purpose of my life?" This next question hit me in the head like a big rock: "What is the purpose of my life?"

I remember meditating and asking this question again and again. I guess I wanted to attain and gain more, but in reality, nothing was enough to satisfy my hunger and empty soul. I suppose that was when Mother Mary came to my rescue. And thank God, what perfect timing!

Chapter 1

What is the Name?

WHAT IS THE NAME?

It was in 2006, at 8 o'clock in the morning, an overcast Saturday morning at Coogee Beach, Sydney, Australia, when I saw an apparition of our Blessed Virgin Mary. An unforgettable experience that changed my whole life. The rebirth of my faith in my Catholic religion. I am thankful to God that I was grace enough to see Her and gifted to change. What a total transformation! I went from a lukewarm believer to a total believer, from a sinner to a less sinful person, trying my utmost best to do the right thing by being an active practising believer.

I lived in Coogee, walking distance from the beach. Almost every morning, I walked around the beach, and that particular morning, I went to see the photo of one of the Bali bombing victims, which I found floating near Coogee's seashore. Whose photo, was it? I do not know but I put it back on top of the hill in Dodley Park where the Bali Bombing Shrine is. I knew it belonged there. Every now and again I go up there and check the same photo, making sure it was still intact on the wall and not blown away again.

To my surprise, all the victim's photos with their names are now permanently imprinted on a wall plaque, never to be blown away. I also found out that the photo which I was looking after belongs to Adam L Howard. Since Adam's photo and identity were safe, I decided to say a few prayers for him and all the victims. I went to pray at the railing, looking over at the water. As I was praying, I notice a big cloud formation of a veil which looked exactly like Blessed Mary's veil on the sky. My focus at this time was on the veil in the sky, and I saw clearly the face of our Blessed Virgin Mother Mary up in the sky in front of me.

I was in awe. I did not know what to say, but all I could utter was, "Oh, my God," repeatedly as I made the sign of the cross. Mama Mary was smiling, and she looked so beautiful and very young.

Am I dreaming or hallucinating? I couldn't help but think. I knew I was not, as I pinched the back of my left hand and felt aware of what was happening.

Similarly, to this apparition in Fatima and Lourdes. She looked like she was saying something, but I could not hear anything. I asked Her to make it louder as I am a little deaf in my right ear. But there was no response.

Then, maybe I thought she was not talking to me; maybe she was talking to someone behind my back. But no one was there except me.

Then a prompting came to me to just relax and enjoy Mama Mary's presence, which I did. It would have taken around three to four minutes looking at our mother in awe and wonder.

WHAT IS THE NAME?

It took me a while to recover from that encounter, and I was doubtful and confused. Should I tell my family and close friends about my whole experience?

I hesitated to tell anyone as they might think I was going crazy or making up a story.

Internally, I struggled and affirm that I believe in telling the truth. Why should I waste theirs and my time by telling false stories? What will I gain from it?

The truth will always come out. This experience was a big deal for me, and I want to share it with others. But how?

Several days had passed and I was still unsure whether to tell anybody about my life-changing experience. Then one day, I remember a year ago when Sister Angeline Lopez invited me to join them to a Cenacle group, a place for families who pray the rosary together. The group will have the statue of the Blessed Mary circulated from house to house, where families pray the rosary, modelling the vigil of Mother Mary and Jesus Apostles in the upper room in Jerusalem. I refused her invitation as I was so busy with work and did not have time for the family rosary. I didn't even pray the rosary by myself then. But now, after the miracle, it was a different story. I immediately rang Sister Angeline and told her my miracle, and we both agreed to bring the Statue of the Blessed Virgin Mary on the 8th of December 2006 and had a mass celebrated in my unit. And that was the start of my devotion and saying the rosary every day to Her. It was then that the Coogee Family Cenacle Group was born so was my faith rebirth.

Since I am an amateur landscape oil painter, I decided to try and paint the spot where I saw Her, as shown here. Imagine me standing on the railings looking at the sky. Unfortunately, I did not do much justice to her beautiful face as I am not good at portrait painting.

WHAT IS THE NAME?

Chapter 2

What is Penance?

WHAT IS PENANCE?

After the 8th of December 2006, I learnt what penance was all about. Mama Mary's statue was in my place up in Coogee as the start of my Family Cenacle prayer group. She will be with me for two weeks before moving on. Since she is visiting me, I thought I must treat her with the utmost respect and make her feel at home, like we do with our visitors. I pray the rosary every day and talk to her.

One day, after my walk on the beach, I got home and made myself a cup of coffee. Whilst I was making it, I was talking to Mama Mary. I said, "Mother Mary, I hear about this penance that we have to do. I wonder what it is that I have to do." I was then prompted to open the blue book, which is The Marian Movement of Priest. I opened the book and found it was about penance. It was so surprising that I did not even look at the table of contents. This book is one and a half inches thick. I find it unbelievable, but it happened. With just one flick of my finger, I turned to the page about penance. For me, Mama Mary is alive and always there to answer my prayers, request and questions. She is with me all the time, and it sounds spooky, but I love it, and I love her so dearly.

I always believe what God promises in the Bible: Ask and you will receive; Seek and you will find; knock and it will be opened for you.

One day, I asked Mama Mary to please give me a sign of my expiration here on earth. It sounds like a very silly question, but I thought *maybe I could get an answer*. I truly believe what Jesus said; Ask and you will receive. I asked Mama Mary to give me at least 6 months before my expiration date so I will be prepared. I can't remember how I come about August is my expiration date, which was just around the corner, and about 3 months before expiration I asked for an extension as I had not finished my book, my will and all the things I must do. I asked seriously, "What to do?" I said maybe she could give me a sign again that August is my real expiration date or maybe I can extend it since I am not ready yet.

The following day, I got the sign again. I smiled and thanked her for answering my question. Now, the question that left me so confused was whether the sign she gave me was my expiration day or an extension because I had not finished the things I was supposed to finish.

I have now learnt my lesson when asking Mama Mary. I must be:

1. Very clear and precise with my questions.
2. I will write it down so I can go back to it, see my questions for myself, and not blame her if she gives me a wrong reply or answer to my request, prayer, and questions.

To recap, penance is an act of self-mortification or devotion performed voluntarily to show sorry for sins or other wrongdoings.

WHAT IS PENANCE?

According to the "Our Lady Queen of Peace at Medjugorje" booked by Michael Henegham, Mother Mary wants us to do penance on Wednesday and Friday. Learning this, I now offer not to have coffee the whole day every Wednesday and Friday. I find it hard as I am used to having my coffee daily, first thing in the morning.

Not so much of a penance but I commit myself to it and I offer this sacrifice to Mama Mary not so much for myself but for anybody who needs help.

I believe that when we offer our prayers, penance, and/or sacrifices to our Lady, she collects them all and distributes them. That is, she gives them to people and souls in Purgatory who need just a few more prayers to reach heaven. In other words, they reach heaven sooner than they wait for people whom they knew or relied on for prayers to help them get there.

Mama Mary uses our prayers, penance and sacrifices to help these souls, and once these souls are in heaven, they, in return, help us down here on earth. How good is that?

I am not for certain if it is a true case as I have not experience it. I just learnt this from some talks, seminars and/or readings which I have done before which I can't remember which, when and where I got them from;

Chapter 3

Miracle of Obedience

MIRACLE OF OBEDIENCE

There is something in me that always looks for some "freebie" such as information, books, or readings on tables located in front of the churches that I visit. So one day, I picked up a small booklet titled, "Our Lady Queen of Peace of Medjugorje". On page 14 of this booklet, it says that "Our Blessed Mother Mary says 'For Christmas Day, I wish that every family of the parish should bring a flower as a sign of adoration to Jesus.' I wish that every family member has a flower placed next to the crib so that Jesus can come and see your devotion to Him." To me, that makes sense since it is Jesus who is the one celebrating his birthday on Christmas Day, and I think he deserves even more than a flower.

(By the way, I fully submit to the final ruling of the Catholic Church on the authenticity of the alleged appearances of Our Lady at Medjugorje).

I remember that on the 24th of December 2006, I was invited to a Christmas Eve dinner at a friend's place near Dural. It was a great gathering with lots of food and exchanging of gifts. It was around 11:30 pm when a couple who are also friends of mine decided that they wanted to hear the midnight Mass. Since the party was finishing, I thought I would rather go with them to hear Mass. On the way out, near the house's entrance, I saw a plant with beautiful white flowers, which reminded me of the wish of the Blessed Mary about the flowers to give to Jesus, so I asked my friend who owned the house for some flowers. She gladly permitted me to help myself, and this I did without hesitation. I gathered some flowers and gave some to Susan and her boyfriend, who were coming with me. I followed their car to the church and it was 11:45 pm when we arrived there. Lots of cars were parked around the church, so we had to park a distance away and walk back. Whilst walking toward the church, I saw the same plant with lots of flowers along the footpath within my reach. I cut more flowers and gave some to my friend, and she accepted them. The church was jam-packed and more people were coming in. I thought, *there is no way can I offer these flowers to Jesus.*

People were gathering outside the church and you had to squeeze yourself to even get in. But then a strange man, unknown to me, nicely dressed in a beige long-sleeve shirt approached me and asked.

"How many are you?"

I quickly replied, "Three".

"Follow me," he said, which we did. We walked with him straight to the front of the altar where three seats were waiting for us. I thought, *that was lucky.* In front and under the altar, I saw the big nativity scene and, of course, the crib with Jesus. I thought it would be best to offer the flowers to Jesus so I don't have to carry it with me. But before I could even go close to the crib, the music began to play and the priest with his entourage walked in, and everybody stood up. By this time, the priest was in front whilst the people were singing while still standing up.

I received an urgent prompting: "Now. Now. Now." It grew louder and louder. So, I stood in front of the crib and offered the flowers to baby Jesus. My friend followed me with her bunch of flowers as well. It felt like we were part of the Mass celebration.

Then the Mass started. I was shivering with what I had just done in front of the whole congregation, which, as far as I knew, had never been done before. It was as if we were part of the start of the Mass. I think Mother Mary had something to do with what had happened so that people would do the same every Christmas day, flowers for baby Jesus.

The following year, when I went to hear Mass at Coogee on Christmas day, I was surprised to see two girls giving flowers to people coming into the church. These flowers were to be offered during the start of the Mass, but nevertheless, I had brought my own flower for Baby Jesus.

Chapter 4

The Miracle of Courage

THE MIRACLE OF COURAGE

On the 14th of January 2007, I was invited to the wedding of my friend's daughter in La Fontana Restaurant at Leichhardt. It was a well-organised wedding and I had a great time seeing old familiar faces again. There was scrumptious food and lots of laughing and dancing. It was done in a venue that finishes at a set time which was midnight. I thought I would leave a bit early since I live in Coogee and it would take at least thirty minutes without traffic to get home. I bid farewell to everyone and off I went. I drove home safely, considering I was a bit sleepy and tired.

I arrived at my place just before midnight. I live in a secure block of buildings, where you have to open your car window to scan your card so the garage roller door of the building opens. As I did that and waited for it to open fully, I noticed a car behind mine and a man getting out on the passenger side. He ran towards my car. From my side mirror, all I could see was his silhouette, completely black.

I thought he would probably ask me something. To my great surprise he said, "Give me your key." Hearing this command, I automatically held on to my keys tighter. The first thing that came into my mind was, 'Fear not says the Lord.'

I stared into his eyes in his balaclava-covered face. I noticed the gun pointed at my face and shouted, "No," and then a long and louder, "Nooooo!" His left hand the one without the gun, with its black gloves pressed on my hand which was trying to firmly hold on to the key. His grip was so strong that my hand was hurting, so I had to pull my hands out from his strong grip and thus let go of the key. As I pulled my hand away from holding the key, I noticed the car slightly move so I positioned the gear to Park. Doing such, had the unintentional result because he could pull the key out of the ignition.

He ran off with my car key, and I thought he was gone. All this had taken about one and a half minutes. I then started shouting for help continuously at the top of my voice.

I wished someone would shout or make a noise to deter this culprit, but no one was there to help me. Surprisingly, the same man came back, was on the other side of my car, and demanded I open the door.

At that time, I thought, *He does not know how to use my late model Mercedes car key* (it does not look like a key but press the button ones). This does not look like an ordinary or standard key you just put into a hole to open. This time I thought, *Oh no! He is after my bag and my mobile phone.* I immediately grabbed my handbag, my mobile phone and new shoes which I had taken off as they were hurting my feet. I was holding my shoes and was ready to throw them at him if he happened to open my car door. Unable to open the door, made him frustrated. So he broke the window glass using the back of the gun. Broken glass was smashed all over the car while I ducked to cover and protect my face. Before I knew it, I saw the other man at the back car waving at him. They left and I was so relieved they were gone. I was so shaken and traumatised by the experience. I immediately went to my mobile phone to call the police by dialling triple zero. Before I even pressed the 0, the security guards from the neighbouring building were around my car.

Where were you a minute ago? I thought. The police, the ambulance and the fire department were soon there too. I was taken to Maroubra Police Station for a statement, and my car was taken the following day for forensic tests. The incident was on the news and the radio the following morning. I was shaken with what had happened and the thought of what could have happened to me. And then there was the constant thoughts of: Should I have done this? Or that?

I truly thank God for the strength and courage to endure this episode in my life. The best thing was the wisdom to think quickly and not to fear—"FEAR NOT, SAYS THE LORD!" What could have happened if I had not followed that?

It took me one month to overcome the shock of it and feel safe again. It was then that I found out that my attacker received twenty years imprisonment for seven charges for carjacking and similar offences, including shooting a policeman who luckily did not die.

Isaiah 41:10

"Fear not, says the Lord, for I am with you; be not dismayed, for I am your God;

I will strengthen you, I will help you, I will uphold you with my righteous right hand."

Chapter 5

Miracle of Blessing

MIRACLE OF BLESSING

On our tour of Israel in October 2011, we visited Jerusalem, where people worship and pray. (It is called the "Wailing Wall" of the former Temple.) It is a big stone wall on which people can write their wishes and pray to God that their wishes come true.

When I found out, I hurriedly looked for a piece of paper to write my wish on and stuck it on the wall. I can clearly remember what I wrote on the paper: "May I find a house before Christmas." I then prayed and stuck the paper on the Wailing Wall.

I had been looking for a house to move into for more than two and a half years but I'd had no luck in finding one that would suit me and my budget. I remember looking at one in Lilyfield in September and I liked it and put an offer lower than the highest auction bid. The agent laughed at my offer and said that the owner would not even accept anything less than a million dollars. It was not known to me that the property had been at auction and the highest bidder of 900K was not accepted. Yet here I was, offering a much lower price. However, I was adamant to the agent that he just put the offer in.

I had not heard from the agent since September, so I just forgot about it. On 24 December 2011, I received a call from the agent stating that my offer had been accepted at my bargain price. I was so happy that I could afford to have my own house.

Before Christmas, I now had my own new house, and this was the exact date I had written on my wish, which I had stuck in the Wailing Wall.

God works in miraculous ways; I truly believe He made this thing to happen.

Thank God He listens and gives us what we need and ask for. He is always there for us, as He promised. Again, I asked, and He answered at His own time, which was the date of my request.

God is so good. Never ever think twice in asking the Lord.

Chapter 6

Miracle of Wonder

COMPASSION AND CARE

MIRACLE OF WONDER

Imagine going to the toilet and seeing that there is no toilet paper. Don't you just dislike it when you see that no toilet paper is provided? This happened to me in my sister's house in the Philippines.

Of course, I shouted, "Sis, where is your toilet paper?"

She yelled back, "There are toilet rolls inside the cabinet."

"Thank you," I answer back.

After finishing up in the toilet and washing my hands, I was looking for hand paper towel.

In desperation, I asked again, "May I have a paper towel?"

"What paper towel?" she replied. "We do not have that."

"What do you mean?" I asked as I pulled the wet paper towel from my pocket. I had used it to wipe my tears while talking to my brother, who was in Sydney, via Skype.

"Look," I showed her, "you gave me this upstairs."

"I have not been upstairs, and I did not give you that."

"Who gave this to me, then?" I insistently asked her.

"I don't know who gave you that, as no one is here and we do not have nor use paper towel here," she replied.

"Who was here?" I asked, more insistently.

"No one except YaYa," she replied. YaYa was the name of the housemaid who was looking after her daughter. They were all downstairs, and nobody had gone upstairs since.

"Somebody handed this to me. Since I was focusing on my conversation with our brother, I did not even look to see who gave it to me. I just grabbed it."

"Tell me what happened?" my sister asked.

"I was upstairs, sitting in front of the computer, talking via Skype to Chito," I started. He was telling me how he was going to donate land he inherited from our late Auntie to Saint Rita Colleges so they could build more orphanages on it. I was crying, tears falling down my cheeks, and then this paper towel was given to me. I was so engrossed with the conversation that I did not even say 'thank you' to the giver."

I took a breath before continuing. "From my side vision, I notice a beige long dress beside me. I did not worry about it as I thought someone in the house. After our chat, I was busting to go to the toilet, that is why I went hurriedly downstairs and went straight in the bathroom."

MIRACLE OF WONDER

"It was definitely not me or any of us that went upstairs to give you that, we do not have that kind of paper towel here in my house," my sister confirmed and pointing at the paper towel saturated in tears as I showed it to her.

Who do you think gave me the paper towel? I asked myself. Could it be my guardian angel, who could not bear to see my tears destroy the computer. Or for me to remember the incident of my brother's word of donating his land to Saint Rita's College for an orphanage.

There is something in this Angel and Saint experience yet to unfold and to continue.

Chapter 7
Alicia's Revelation

ALICIA'S REVELATION

Today, I decided to type my experience after our Divine Mercy two-day silent retreat that went from the 30th of November to the 1st of December 2013, in Mount Carmel Retreat Centre in Varroville, NSW. Silent retreat meant there was no talking for two days, no mobile phones, etc. Just praying and talking to Jesus. Our agenda included Mass, Adoration, Rosary, Meditations, and Reflections. There were also Priest presentations and lectures.

On the first day of the retreat, we attended a mass and adoration afterwards. We were told to stay and pray or go to our room to rest. It was just 10 am, so I decided to stay and pray in front of the Blessed Sacrament. In my meditation that time, I clearly remember what I said to Jesus. I said, "Jesus, I have seen your Mother, and how I wish I could see you too." Then, the rest of my chatter about my days. When I talk to Jesus and Mama Mary, I talk to them as if they are my close friends, listening to me intently. I loved it as I voiced my joy, thanksgiving, complaints and everything that happened to me that I could remember at the time. That was my way of adoration, to just sit there in the presence of the Lord. There are many occasions that I got an answer through the Holy Spirit, I guess.

Like my other miracles, I thought, *I better write it down so I can pass it around just in case I forget.* At least it is already in my book of revelations, as I want to call it. After the completion of the silent retreat, we were told to gather in the dining room to break the silence and share the afternoon tea they had prepared for us. It was around 4 pm when I went pass the dining area and didn't see many people there. I decided to go and pack my bag as we had to be out of our rooms at around 5 pm, so at least I would not be hurrying and could just relax and socialise with ease.

There were around twenty-three retreatants from different places who attended.

A Filipina lady approached me and started talking about her trip to Medjugorie, and since I had been there as well, we had a wonderful conversation.

I do not remember what brought about our conversation when I started telling her about seeing Mama Mary in Coogee—I just tell my miracle experiences to people without due reason. She was questioning me as to which Blessed Virgin Mary I saw: Lourdes, Medjugorie, Guadalupe, or Fatima. I told her the one with the blue veil, which she thought was Fatima.

At this stage Annie, who was the sister of Ruby, who organises our retreat. She joined our conversation and Maury told her that I saw the Blessed Virgin Mary at Coogee. Annie responded straight away, "Have you seen the miracle of the sun?" and we both said "No."

The sun was blasting at the time (around 5 pm). Annie, at this stage, asked us to wait, and she quickly called Ruby; they asked Maury and me to go quietly with them outside so they could show us the Miracle of the Sun. They both pray over us, meaning they put their hands above our heads in prayer, and I closed my eyes to solemnly listen to their prayers. Then they ask us to open our eyes and look at the sun. Without any hesitation, I opened my eyes and saw the sun set back. It was not shining bright.

Beside and just in front of the sun, was a big, black cross.

I was so astounded that I cried repeatedly, "Oh my God, there is the cross, there is the cross!" In my excitement, I guess I was getting too loud, as Ruby told me, "Not too loud, Alicia," as the other retreat guests might all come out.

I was still totally excited to see the cross and kept saying, 'Oh my God' repeatedly when I thought I wanted to see the cross again. So I decided to look at the sun for a second time, but this time I saw a silhouette of God (not sure who it was as I couldn't see His face). His arms were stretched out, just like when we welcome someone from afar. In my great excitement, I also outstretched my arms widely, my heart pounding with extreme joy as I exclaimed, "Oh my God." (As I type this revelation, tears are gushing from my eyes, just like they did after I saw God).

This all happened in a few seconds, as you cannot look at the sun for too long, as it could harm your eyes. I then closed my eyes, with warm excitement still simmering in me and "Oh, my God" escaping my lips.

Next thing I knew, Annie was asking us what we saw and she was telling us what God was telling her, that He will be there for us on the hour of our death. My excitement was so intense that what Annie was telling me was not registering in my brain clearly. I even missed out hearing about Maury's experience and what she saw.

Afterwards, Maury, Annie and I went back in the dining room. I remember saying to Maury, "Can you see? My eyesight is a bit dim." Blink, blink, blink, and in a few seconds, my normal vision was back. I did not have a chance to talk to Annie and Maury as everybody was rushing to go home. I thought I would try to meet up with them someday and relive the experience. I also thought I should paint what I saw.

In Luke10:21-24: Jesus says to his disciples, "Blessed are the eyes that see what you see.

For I say to you, many Prophets and Kings desired to see but did not see it and hear what you hear but did not hear it."

I again thank God for answering my wish to see Him. At times I question myself, who am I, and why did He showed Himself to me? All I know, He is a very loving God and does not discriminate or judge anybody I asked and He answered me.

ALICIA'S REVELATION

Chapter 8

Miracle of Heaven and Hell

FLIGHT TO MIAMI

MIRACLE OF HEAVEN AND HELL

There are times when things happen to us for a reason. I can clearly remember what happened to me on board American Airline plane on my flight from Los Angeles to Miami USA on the 9th of July 2015.

As always, when you board a plane, you look for your seat. Mine was 29C. I sat down and waited for takeoff. Sitting on the aisle, the next seat to me was still vacant, and a lady was near the window. I noticed that the lady seated close to the window was crying.

My inquisitive mind wanted to know why she was crying. My heart told me to help, console or support her. So, I asked, "Hi, are you okay? Why are you crying?"

She answered me in a sobbing voice, "I cannot help myself; this book makes me very, very sad."

I asked, "What book is that?" She showed me the book, and I quickly registered its name in my mind: "My Time in Heaven" by Richard Sigmund. Unable to say anything else, the next thing I knew, a woman stood in the aisle in front of me and said, "You are seated in my seat 26C."

I was adamant that I was seated in the right seat, so I quickly looked for my boarding pass to check. However, I found out I was wrong. I was supposed to sit three rows further up. I apologised for my mistake, and I immediately said 'goodbye' to the crying lady and left her.

This incident did not happen randomly, nor is it a coincidence. When I got to Los Angeles, California, I looked for the book, but it was not available in any book shop there unless you ordered it. So, when I got back to Sydney, I decided to order it in Dymocks.

I read the book and enjoyed the beauty, peace and love in heaven. Whilst reading about heaven, I did not cry at all. That time it seems, I was reading in search of that crying part which the lady in the plane was crying about. Then I got to the chapter on 'Hell' and I was crying, all right. I had almost finished a full box of tissues because I was so affected and sad over what I read. The effect on me was tremendous. Then I assumed that, that was the part the lady was reading when I saw her.

After reading the book; I promised myself I would do my best in all my capacity here on earth to avoid hell for myself and others. I would try my best to tell others the story of how I got hold of that book and why it was important to have the idea about Heaven and Hell. This is a serious business as we all do not know when, where and how we are going to die. Whether we like it or not, we are going to go. I would definitely want to go to Heaven and be blessed with eternal life. That is of course passing purification which is Purgatory for clean-up. We all have expiration dates, only God knows when it is. So, we have to always be ready 24/7. There are many passages in the Holy Bible that says for us to be prepared for the coming of the Lord. One of the most well known is in Matthew 24:44, which reads: "Therefore, you also must be ready for the Son of Man is coming at an hour you do not expect."

One day, I was enjoying playing with my iPad clicking on You tube, I thought, why not search for Richard Sigmund which I did. To my surprise, his story was in "You Tube" – "A Place called Heaven/Near Death Experience" 1 hour and 18 mins. Wow his description of heaven in his books was similar as he narrated it in You Tube.

On YouTube, I'm surprised to discover more testimonies about experiences like Don Piper's "90 Minutes in Heaven – The True Story That Happened to Don Piper." Video of 1:07 minutes features Dean Braxton's "Greatest Heaven Visit Testimony," which runs for 1 hour and 45 minutes. There's also Bill Wiese's testimony about his twenty-three minutes in Hell. To me, that proves beyond any doubt that Heaven and Hell exist. I notice there are striking similarities in their accounts of what they saw in Heaven and Hell.

Now that I am sure there is Heaven and Hell, I will do my utmost best to achieve to go to Heaven and not even think of the possibility of going to Hell. I am so grateful to God for my divine intervention in the plane on my flight to Miami.

Through this intervention, I also learnt to never ignore others who need help, support or a shoulder to cry on. Like the good Samaritan in the Gospel of Luke 10:25-37 where a Samaritan help a man who was attacked and left almost dead on the road, unlike a priest and a Levite who just passed by ignoring the man. This is a very popular parable of Jesus where love, compassion and mercy were profoundly emphasized.

Chapter 9

Miracle of Devotion

MIRACLE OF DEVOTION

Hearing Mass almost every day for thirty minutes brings me true happiness and joy in life. I make an effort to say hello to our Heavenly Father, Jesus, Holy Spirit, Blessed Virgin Mary, and all the angels and Saints.

I go to St Joseph's Church in Camperdown.

For me, the Holy Eucharist is my way to be with God face to face and receive Him in my heart daily. It is the sacrament of transubstantiation, which happens during the consecration of the Mass. This is when the bread and wine truly become the body, blood, soul, and divinity of our Lord Jesus Christ.

Also, it is my way of listening, understanding and remembering His daily words through the Holy Scriptures and Gospels, which are being explained by the priest.

Knowing what God says in the scriptures is what God teaches us and what He wants us to do and follow. For me, I take it as the basis of my life. Through it, Jesus gave us lots of practical stories/ parables that we can follow, which I love. All I do is remember and practice it daily in action. Be an active listener and active action taker/participant.

One day for whatever reason I was running late. I knew I would be late, which I tried not to as a practice of self-discipline not to be late, which I am forever trying to do.

In my rush, I spoke to God, saying these exact words: "Lord, please wait for me."

I would have been late, around fifteen mins for mass, but when I got there, I saw everybody standing outside the church as if waiting for the door to open.

I asked my friend Loura who normally opened the church, what is happening. She said her keys to open the church, which she always used, were not working, so she asked Father Anthony, our Parish Priest at the time, to open the church. Father tried his keys in front and at the back door and they did not work either.

When I arrived, I saw Father. I waved to him, which he reciprocated, and tried his keys again to open the front door. This time, miraculously, it opened. I knew exactly what had happened, but I was not game to tell anyone. God answered my prayer to wait for me. The church did not open until I got there. God listened to me. Nothing is impossible with God. His will is done.

I am so grateful to God for granting my wishes, but I will never do that again. Wishing for my own good only is selfish. What about the inconvenience I caused others?

For me, I truly and wholeheartedly believe that God will always give us what we ask for, or even better, if He wills it at His own time. I have to be aware and precise about what

MIRACLE OF DEVOTION

I ask for from God. He so loves us all, He will give us what we ask for. I will never forget that passage in **Matthew 7:7-8:** *"Ask and it will be given to you; seek, and you will find; knock and it will be opened to you. For everyone who asks receives and he who seeks finds, and to him who knocks it will be opened."*

Chapter 10
Miracle of Giving

MIRACLE OF GIVING

My life has been amazing. Sometimes, even without asking, God knows what we need and gives it to us. He is an all-giving God.

One day, on my way home from church, I remembered that I needed to get some milk, so I quickly pulled over my car when I saw a small corner store. As I was getting my purse from my bag, I realised I left it at home. So here I was, digging for some coins in my bag. I then realised that I could have some tacked in the glove compartment of my car. I decided to get out of the car so it would be easier to look for the coins on the other side since it was on the passenger side. As I got out, I saw a Hundred-dollar bill on the ground. I looked around first just in case someone had dropped it, but no one was there, so I picked it up and Thank God for a hundred dollars to buy the milk. I still looked at the glove compartment and got some coins out to buy the milk. I was not using the one-hundred-dollar bill for that.

Come the following Sunday, they are asking donation for Tsunami victims in church.

So, I put the hundred-dollar bill in a donation envelope and handed it in. I am so happy about that, and I am sure God would be happy, too.

Imagine the happiness you feel when someone gives you something, whether in goods or help. Also, imagine how you feel when you help others. For me, the intensity of my happy feeling is greater when I have helped others, even in the smallest way. I tap myself on the shoulder and say to myself, "That is your good Samaritan job for the day."

I will never forget the movie I watched, "Pay It Forward," starring Kevin Spacey and Helen Hunt. In that film, I learned that kindness to others has a ripple effect. In other words, one good deed can inspire others to help as well. Also, true kindness is selfless; when we assist others without expecting a reward, our actions become meaningful. Helping others and encouraging them to help in return can have a massive impact on our world. Even a simple smile and kind words can make a big difference to how others feel.

Why not try doing it every day and see how it will impact others?

Matthew 25:40

"Truly I say to you, as you did it to one of the least of these my brethren, you did it to me." Meaning when we help others in need we are serving Him.

Chapter 11

Miracle Signs

READINESS AND REASSURANCE

MIRACLE SIGNS

It has been my intention to find out how to go to heaven. As we all know, we are only temporary residents of earth. We are lucky to live to 100 years old. Since I am close to my expiration date, and I don't know when, where, or how God will call me, I better prepare myself and my soul.

After reading Richard Sigmund's book My Time in Heaven and watching several videos on YouTube about heaven, hell, and purgatory, I believe there is no better place to go than Heaven. We are going to eternal life. It is paradise. God made and prepared the very best for all of us. He loves us so much. He wants us all to be saints. God wants us to be there with Him, along with all the angels and the saints.

How do I get to Heaven? What I have to do is always a question in my mind. What does God want me to do? What is my mission on earth, my purpose? All these questions boil to one answer, and the best way is to follow Jesus Christ, but How, I may ask. To follow Him is to learn about what He did and His life here on earth. To replicate his actions, words and deeds. So, get the Holy Bible, which I consider the manual of our life on how to live here on earth, handed to us from generation to generation, written over 2000 years ago. This book is where the words of our Lord were written, He wants us to read, remember and follow. And of course, actively practice it in our daily lives. God wants us to love Him and love our neighbours as we love ourselves.

Considering all that, I thought following it would be the surest way to heaven. One day, I visited my mum in her house. I always bond well with my mum. She is the best person, mother, and friend to me. Her love is kind, forgiving, and unconditional, no matter what you do. She always welcomes me, like everybody else, with open arms. This particular day was different. She cooked our lunch.

During lunch, we had a serious chat about inheritance. We talked about my great-grandmother's inheritance to us and how we felt about it. Then we discussed where my grandmother would be—in Heaven or still in purgatory being cleaned. My mum says this about my grandmother: "Her being religiously going to church twice daily, she would definitely be in Heaven by now. And plus, all my mum's praying the rosary for her intentions."

I also added that, because of her great generosity and kindness to us and many others, she would be in heaven by now.

I don't know what came to me when I told my mum that if she went to heaven, she would give me a sign. She just giggled with what I said and replied, "Don't be silly".

Then I continued, "If I go first and you pray the rosary for me daily, and when I get to heaven, I will definitely give you a sign that I am there already." Then we gave each other a "High Five", a childlike sign of agreement.

MIRACLE SIGNS

I believe that people on earth pray for souls in purgatory. The more people pray for your soul, the shorter you stay in Purgatory, and then you move to Heaven. How true that is, I really do not know, but I promised to tell you with a sign when I get there.

My mum and I kind of agreed on our promise, but only verbally.

On the 19th of December 2012, my mum passed away at the age of eighty-three due to health complications. Since then, I have been praying the rosary daily, offering it for her and all the souls in purgatory through the Blessed Virgin Mary's intercessions.

One day, I went home late and was too tired to go to bed. I told my mum in prayer that I would pray the rosary for her the following day.

I got myself ready for bed until I remembered I had to tell my friend a few important things. So, I started texting my friend. Whilst I was doing that, the photo of my mum pop up on my phone. I got thousands of photos and to get her photo's up is merely impossible. Immediately, I thought my mum wanted me not to miss praying the rosary. I also told her to let me know if she is already in heaven. As I thought and suspected that she would be counting the days before she went to heaven.

I clearly remember that, half a year later, the same photo popped up again on my phone, and I assumed that was her sign that she was already in heaven. Nevertheless, I still included her in my rosary prayers until now.

Chapter 12

Miracle of Love and Sufferance

MIRACLE OF LOVE AND SUFFERANCE

On the 4th of April 2009, I finally found out what love was all about. It only took me sixty-one years to understand and work on it.

I clearly remember when I asked Sister Angeline (my sister in Christ, mentor and best friend) "Why she and hundreds of people do the things they do in helping other people. They go out of their way without getting paid to help people, do charitable work, give their time to listen, money and assistance," she said. "It all voids down to LOVE." She says everything we do is for Love; God wants us to Love our neighbours as ourselves. Written as the 2nd Commandment of God handed down to us through Moses in Mount Sinai. Yes, I do believe that but I cannot understand the logic of it. Why do they go out of their way to help complete strangers/people who they hardly know? For me it is a bit weird not being selfish, to give love and time to someone I do not love. I am thick about this but I just can not comprehend. It is too hard for me to see the logic of why saints like St. Francis de Assisi gave up this rich, beautiful life to give it all to the poor. Same as Mother Theresa and other saints as well.

As one of my friends commented, helping and caring for others, like Sis Angeline and Legion of Mary, are useless causes, as he reasons that you cannot make money from them. For him, what a waste. For him, it was a waste of time and effort. He also justifies that if you give money to the poor, you make them poorer, for they will just rely on handouts all the time. He added that you only make them poor for the rest of their lives. I totally agree in a way, but not all people are users of other people's charitable nature. Some disadvantage people only need help until they can stand on their own feet. That is when we tried to help them.

When I die, all I want is to enter Heaven, to see the Blessed Virgin Mary, Jesus Christ, all the angels and saints, my families, and all my friends. I can only do that if I follow Jesus and what he did here on earth. He says, "FOLLOW ME TO ENTER THE KINGDOM OF GOD." So now I am trying to find a strategic, easy way to go to heaven.

My prayer is, "Lord, teach me how to follow you to enter your kingdom." So, I read the bible with the little time I got. I also read God's Word Daily Reflection, which is short, understandable and with reflection and I can get the idea of how Jesus lived His life and tried to copy it the best I can in my own humble way.

Some weekends I spend time with our Cenacle (Marian Praying) group seminar (praying, chatting, socialising). Given 5-10 minutes by our co-ordinator, I will share my experience of seeing the Blessed Virgin Mary. It is important that I was given the mission to tell others how my apparition happened. I really do wish they believe it. I am just telling what I truly and honestly saw. I felt so privileged and honoured that the Blessed Virgin Mary showed herself to me. At first, I was very hesitant to tell anybody about my story, but I realised there was a reason for all this. I sometimes wonder, why me, is it because I hate telling lies and it is my principle in life to always only tell the truth and nothing but the truth.

Jesus gave His life for His love for us. This is huge. Love for the whole human race. My life, my principles and my love that I am willing to give and offer is so small compare to what Jesus has given us. No comparison. Jesus suffered on the cross for our salvation. That is love and that love have sufferance. So, to follow Jesus, what sufferance do I have to do to show my love?

I really fear public speaking. I would rather be a listener, but I have to learn to speak in public so I can convey the message I want to impart to others. That message, for me, is suffering and love of God and the Blessed Virgin Mary. I suppose if I can pass the message to even one soul, I can bring one soul to Jesus in my own humble way.

Now, I can narrate Love and suffering. I have to suffer to give love. Then I think I cannot find the love of my neighbours because I am not prepared to suffer. I am selfish, and I do not want to give my time to anyone.

Love and suffering go hand in hand. We do things to others because we love them. We give them time, effort and financial help because we love them. Like our children, we give them everything because we love them. We suffer for them; we look after them when they are sick and worried about their welfare and well-being. Love must always have some sort of sufferance without which is not Love.

In our social relationships, we can not find love because we are not prepared to give our time to it. We also have to make sure we get the same treatment and love as we gave them. We do not want to risk our energy and time to learn more about the other person.

Now, I have learned how to suffer when giving love by giving them my time and listening to them. To love unconditionally, I never expect to get anything back in return.

We are all different in showing our love to others. Some show their love through words, some by gifts, some by doing work of kindness, and some just giving prayers and other similar ways. God made us all different in our way of thinking, feeling and reasoning. Not one of us is exactly and completely identical.

We have to know and consider these facts about others so we become more understanding and forgiving in our judgements and ways. In that way, we can truly express our love to others. This is a hard call but if we try to do it with little step at a time.

MIRACLE OF LOVE AND SUFFERANCE

We will gradually become accustomed to giving love to others without effort. It will become second nature to us.

God's ten commandments are divided into two categories. Love God above all things and love your neighbour. He also included to love your neighbour as you love yourself.

Final Chapter

What is Next?

WHAT IS NEXT?

Have you wondered what is the next episode of your life?

After writing this book, I thought that it was my all, my legacy given to humanity based on what God wanted me to do. *That is the purpose of my life.* It happened; it had a beginning and now an ending. The Alpha and Omega, I told them the truth and nothing else, so help me, God.

I become a follower of Jesus, but not just yet. I prayed I wanted to follow His footsteps, no matter what it was. That, for me, is a big, big ask and thinking back, I should not have asked it. I know He came for the salvation of mankind and who am I. Deep in my heart, I knew He knew I could not do it, as I am a scary cat when it comes to dealing with the sick, the dying, the homeless, the vulnerable, and the disabled, like Mother Theresa of Calcutta, who dedicated her life to serving the poorest poor and all of the above. I do not have the sincere love and compassion to give my life to others like some saints, front liners, doctors and social workers who give their all for the service of others. It is so sad and embarrassing to say I am not one of these wonderful unsung heroes.

I mentioned this weakness to my sister in Christ Angeline and other religious friends. I got a clearance and understanding from them that people are called to do what they do. In short, she said, "We all have different purposes and passions in life. We were created by God like that. Mother Theresa, for that purpose, was destined to help the poorest poor, and she absolutely loved doing it. The doctors, nurses and front liners, and each one of us have different jobs, careers and professions. We cannot all have the same destination and purpose in life, she continued.

That makes sense to me, why I cannot do what they are doing, and they cannot do what I am doing. At the end of the day, I guess, God made it that way so we can all be knowledgeable in helping and caring for each other. Who would look after the sick if there were no doctors or nurses? who would be picking up the rubbish bins weekly without the Garbo? What about the dedicated teachers like me who love teaching others and passing my little acquired knowledge and so passionately loving it?

Back to following footsteps for thirty-three years as a human here on earth. I love to heal and help others. All these years of going to attend daily mass and listening to the readings and the gospels and the homily or the explanation of the priest, which could also be called sermon, I have learned and reflected on Jesus' teachings. I considered the Holy Bible our life manual. Like any appliance or household gadget, it has a manual. God created the Bible as a manual for us to read and follow. Everything is in it. Like it says, "If you are worried and burdened, come to Me". It also gave us lots and lots of examples to follow. The best one I have learnt, but I cannot remember where I read it in the bible, was, "God gave us all a healing power." The power to heal comes from God. It is a gift given to us through our faith in the Lord,

WHAT IS NEXT?

prayer and the Holy Spirit. This means we can heal others by praying for them, supporting them, giving them our ears to listen to, our shoulder to cry on, or giving them help to get by. We can physically heal them with our kind words, like the doctors, nurses, caregivers, and helpers.

I guess I can continue following Jesus by healing others in my own capable way and offering it to God. Given the chance and if God's will, I would love to do research and write about how to help others with their sufferings and illnesses. With my knowledge, I can better equip growing children in their development and help families raise their children.

But as for now, God wants me to use my gifts, spread my words, spread my wings and bring others to Him. This was my prompting on the 27th of August 2016, to which I committed myself to Him, and I replied, "Yes, Lord."

THE TRUE MIRACLES OF JESUS

WHAT IS NEXT?

MY DAILY PRAYER

Heavenly Father,
Walk with me today,
And Grant that I may hear
Your Footsteps and
Gladly Follow where they Lead.
Talk with me today
And Grant that I may hear
Your Tender Voice,
And Quicken to Its Counsel.
Stay with me today
And Grant that I may feel Your Gentle Presence
In all I do, say, and think.
Be my Strength when I weaken, my Courage when I fear.
Help me to know that it is Your Hand Holding mine
Through all the hours of this day,
And when night falls,
Grant that I may know I Rest in Your Sacred Heart.

THE TRUE MIRACLES OF JESUS

The Miracle Prayer

Lord Jesus I come before you, just as I am. I am sorry for my sins; I repent of all my sins please forgive me. In your name I forgive all others for what they have done against me. I renounce satan, the evil spirits and all their works. I give you my entire self, Lord Jesus now and forever. I invite you into my life Jesus, I accept you as my Lord, God, and Saviour. Heal me, change me, and strengthen me in body, soul and spirit. Come Lord Jesus, cover me with your precious blood, and fill me with your Holy Spirit. I love you Lord Jesus. I praise you Jesus. I thank you Jesus. I shall follow you every day of my life. Amen

Mary my mother, Queen of Peace, all the Angels and Saints please help me Amen.

Say this prayer faithfully, no matter how you feel. When you come to the point where you sincerely mean each word, with all your heart, something good spiritually will happen to you. You will experience Jesus, and He will change your whole life in very special way. You will see. *(Peter Mary Rookey OSM)*

About the Author

Alicia was born in the Philippines and migrated to Sydney, Australia, in 1975.

She graduated from Lyceum University with a Bachelor of Science in Economics, majoring in Economics. She also earned her Master's degree in Economics from the University of the East in the Philippines.

She works as an executive secretary at Meralco (Manila Electric Company). She also works in PLDT (Phil Long Distance Co). She started her career in Australia as a secretary of the Assistant Registrar at Macquarie University.

She married in 1976 and started her importing company, selling homeware products around Australia.

THE TRUE MIRACLES OF JESUS

In 1987, she invested in a Childcare Centre, where her two children attended. She capitalised on this by making her centre bigger and investing in more properties. She was the licencee, director and educator of her Childcare centre for 37 years.

After being married for twenty-four years and her children living their own lives, she decided to have an amicable divorce,

She began to have a different outlook on life with amazing wealth and freedom. Then she had a realisation and queried herself as to what life is after all. What is next? That was when her rebirth to Catholicism started. When she saw the Blessed Virgin Mary on the 26th of November 2006.

That was the start of her conversion from someone who does not even pray the rosary to daily praying it. She started the Coogee Cenacle (where the image of Mother Mary goes from family to family every two weeks to visit the family and pray the rosary.

During those years, miracles happened in her life. She became close to our Blessed Mother Mary and even closer to Jesus when He showed Himself to her on December 1, 2013. For her, seeing is believing, and from then on, she actively joined the Divine Mercy Reflection Team. Then, she chartered the Divine Mercy Toastmasters Club in Camperdown.

ABOUT THE AUTHOR

She now dedicates her time to volunteering for Church Services. She is the Catechist Coordinator at St Joseph's Church in Camperdown and RCIA (Rite of Christian Initiation of Adults).

Her purpose in life is to be God's light to all and to bring others to God. She believes that sharing her miracle stories will prove that God truly exists and loves us.

Acknowledgement

I would like to thank Sister Angeline Lopez, my best friend, my sister in Christ, and my confidant. She has looked after me while I was undergoing my cancer treatment, and has been my motivator all these years. She also guides me toward my religious beliefs.

I also want to thank my daughter Victoria and my son Charles, and my family who have been incredibly supportive in my trials and tribulations in life.

Testimonials

To Whom It May Concern,

This is to testify that I've known Mrs Alicia Buxton for over thirty-five years. She is a mother of two and adores her two granddaughters. Alice is a fantastic person, she's Godly, hardworking, very kind, witty, very generous and very successful in all that she does. Despite all her trials and tribulations, she passed them all because her attitude in life is positive and she completely surrenders all her ordeal to our creator.

I am full of admiration to this human being and our outstanding friendship, and I wish her all the success in writing her book.

If you wish to know more about her you can contact me on 0419 177 728 .

Best regards,
Amy Cameron

Alicia Buxton is an intelligent, inspiring business woman who has achieved success both in business and in the wider community, through her philanthropic work.

Alicia is a Distinguished Toastmaster and has assisted speakers to find their voice and passion through her mentoring and guidance.

It is an honour to call Alicia both a fellow author and Toastmaster.

Stephanie Giannis, DTM
Entrepreneur, author, Distinguished Toastmaster.

Offers

- Buy one get one book for free.
  (all profit from sales will go to charity)

- Free eBook from every purchase.

- Should you need prayer for you and/or your loved ones, to talk to someone or just a shoulder to cry on, don't hesitate to get in touch with me.

From St. Joseph Catholic Parish Church weekly bulletin.

Alicia Buxton

Alicia Buxton is a child care advocate. She has worked as child care Director and Educator for 37 years. All those years she showed her profound love and care for the children, parents and staff.

Alicia's book is about her life story when she saw the Blessed Virgin Mary on the Twenty Six of November 2006. And Jesus on the 1st of December 2013, which she shared with us.

She shared her story mostly when called upon to share her life experiences in prayer group meetings, parish gatherings and club speeches.

She is a member of Toastmasters International, non profit organization for improving your public speaking and personal growth since 2009.

She chartered/founded Divine Mercy Toastmasters Club in Camperdown NSW in 2015.

She was awarded Canterbury – Business person of the year in 2013 for her business commitment, integrity and leadership.

She was awarded Canterbury Hurlstone Park RSL Club Toastmaster of the year in 2011.

She is an advocate of Evangelisation towards Go Make Disciples.

She wants to actively be the light of God to all.

She is St. Joseph Catholic Church Camperdown – Catechist and RCIA coordinator, which is about children and adults wanting to become a Catholic, Baptise, Confirm and learn about Jesus and the scriptures.

Her goal of writing this book is to make known to others the love of Jesus to us.

Alicia is available and willing to speak about her miracle experiences to support groups, religious organisation and schools.

✉ abuxton333@gmail.com 📞 +61 412 155 967

Notes

THE TRUE MIRACLES OF JESUS

NOTES

www.ingramcontent.com/pod-product-compliance
Lightning Source LLC
Chambersburg PA
CBHW061222070526
44584CB00029B/3947